SUPERHEROES ON A MEDICAL MISSION

# MEDIKIDZ EXPLAIN SLEEP APNEA

P9-AQF-576

rosen publishing's
rosen central®
New York

Dr. Kim Chilman-Blair and Shawn deLoache
Medical content reviewed for accuracy by Dr. Paul Gringras and Dr. David Rapoport

**This edition published in 2011 by:**

The Rosen Publishing Group, Inc.
29 East 21st Street
New York, NY 10010

Additional end matter copyright © 2011 by The Rosen Publishing Group, Inc.

**Library of Congress Cataloging-in-Publication Data**

Chilman-Blair, Kim.
Medikidz explain sleep apnea / Kim Chilman-Blair and Shawn deLoache ; medical content reviewed for accuracy by Paul Gringras and David Rapoport.
    p. cm. — (Superheroes on a medical mission)
Includes bibliographical references and index.
ISBN 978-1-4358-9459-4 (library binding) — ISBN 978-1-4488-1841-9 (pbk.) — ISBN 978-1-4488-1842-6 (6-pack)
1. Sleep apnea syndromes—Comic books, strips, etc—Juvenile literature. I. Deloache, Shawn. II. Title.
RC737.5C55 2011
616.2'09—dc22
                                        2010002554

*Manufactured in China*

CPSIA Compliance Information: Batch #MS0102YA: For further information, contact Rosen Publishing, New York, New York, at 1-800-237-9932.

13

23

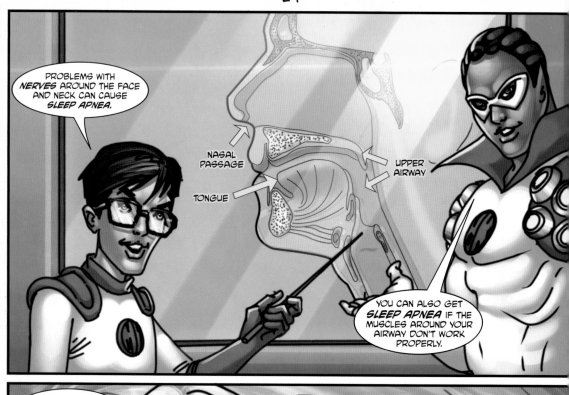

SLEEP APNEA IS MORE COMMON IN OLDER KIDS WHO ARE OVERWEIGHT...

STOMACH, OLD FRIEND, MAYBE IT'S TIME TO LOSE A FEW POUNDS...

HOW COME?

MORE FAT ON YOUR *THROAT* AND *BEHIND YOUR TONSILS* MAKES YOUR AIRWAY NARROWER...

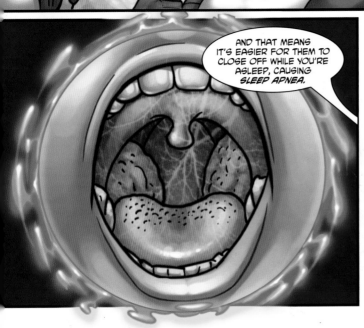

AND THAT MEANS IT'S EASIER FOR THEM TO CLOSE OFF WHILE YOU'RE ASLEEP, CAUSING *SLEEP APNEA.*

IN OLDER KIDS, HEALTHY DIET AND REGULAR EXERCISE HELP TO KEEP *SLEEP APNEA* AT BAY!

LOOK ON THE BRIGHT SIDE, AT LEAST YOU DIDN'T WET THE BED...

...YET.

WET THE BED?!?! ARE YOU KIDDING ME!

GAH!

WELL, IT'S NOBODY'S FAVORITE TOPIC FOR DINNER CONVERSATION, BUT *SLEEP APNEA* CAN SOMETIMES CAUSE BED-WETTING.

I'M GOING TO NEED SOME NEW PANTS.

BUT DON'T WORRY! TREATING SLEEP APNEA CAN HELP WITH THAT.

BAYER, LINDA. *SLEEP DISORDERS*. PHILADELPHIA, PA: CHELSEA HOUSE
PUBLISHERS, 2001.

BRYNIE, FAITH HICKMAN. *101 QUESTIONS ABOUT SLEEP AND DREAMS
THAT KEPT YOU AWAKE NIGHTS... UNTIL NOW.* MINNEAPOLIS, MN:
TWENTIETH-CENTURY BOOKS, 2006.

COVEY, SEAN. *THE 7 HABITS OF HIGHLY EFFECTIVE TEENS PERSONAL
WORKBOOK.* FOREST CITY, NC: FIRESIDE BOOKS, 2003.

ESHERICK, JOAN. *DEAD ON THEIR FEET: TEEN SLEEP DEPRIVATION
AND ITS CONSEQUENCES.* PHILADELPHIA, PA: MASON CREST
PUBLISHERS, 2005.

ESPELAND, PAMELA. *LIFE LISTS FOR TEENS: TIPS, STEPS, HINTS, AND
HOW-TOS FOR GROWING UP, GETTING ALONG, LEARNING, AND
HAVING FUN.* MINNEAPOLIS, MN: FREE SPIRIT PUBLISHING, 2003.

FOLDVERY-SCHAEFER, NANCY. *THE CLEVELAND CLINIC GUIDE TO SLEEP
DISORDERS.* NEW YORK, NY: KAPLAN PUBLISHING, 2009.

FOX, ANNIE. *TOO STRESSED TO THINK? A TEEN GUIDE TO STAYING
SANE WHEN LIFE MAKES YOU CRAZY.* MINNEAPOLIS, MN: FREE
SPIRIT PUBLISHING, 2005.

HIPP, EARL. *FIGHTING INVISIBLE TIGERS: A STRESS MANAGEMENT
GUIDE FOR TEENS.* MINNEAPOLIS, MN: FREE SPIRIT PUBLISHING,
2008.

HIRSHKOWITZ, MAX, AND PATRICIA B. SMITH. *SLEEP DISORDERS FOR
DUMMIES.* HOBOKEN, NJ: WILEY PUBLISHING, INC., 2004.

MACGREGOR, ROB. *DREAM POWER FOR TEENS: WHAT YOUR DREAMS
SAY ABOUT YOUR PAST, PRESENT, AND FUTURE.* CINCINNATI, OH:
ADAMS MEDIA CORPORATION, 2005.

PETERSON, JUDY MONROE. *FREQUENTLY ASKED QUESTIONS ABOUT
SLEEP AND SLEEP DEPRIVATION (FAQ: TEEN LIFE).* NEW YORK, NY:
ROSEN PUBLISHING, 2010.

RENTZ, KRISTEN. *YOGANAP: RESTORATIVE POSES FOR DEEP
RELAXATION.* CAMBRIDGE, MA: DA CAPO PRESS, 2005.

STEINLE, JASON. *UPLOAD EXPERIENCE: QUARTERLIFE SOLUTIONS
FOR TEENS AND TWENTYSOMETHINGS.* EVERGREEN, CO: NASOJ
PUBLICATIONS, 2005.

STEWART, GAIL B. *SLEEP DISORDERS.* SAN DIEGO, CA: LUCENT BOOKS,
2003.

TRUEIT, TRUDI STRAIN. *DREAMS AND SLEEP (LIFE BALANCE).* LONDON,
ENGLAND: FRANKLIN WATTS, 2004.

# INDEX

# ABOUT THE AUTHORS

DR. KIM CHILMAN-BLAIR IS A MEDICAL DOCTOR WITH TEN YEARS OF EXPERIENCE IN MEDICAL WRITING AND A PASSION FOR PROVIDING MEDICAL INFORMATION THAT MAKES CHILDREN WANT TO LEARN.

SHAWN DELOACHE HAS EARNED DEGREES IN PSYCHOLOGY AND CRIMINAL JUSTICE FROM THE UNIVERSITY OF GEORGIA IN ATHENS, GEORGIA. HE HAS WORKED WITH CHILDREN AS A COUNSELOR, TEACHER, AND MARTIAL ARTS INSTRUCTOR, AND CURRENTLY WORKS WITH SPECIAL NEEDS CHILDREN. HE MOVED TO NEW YORK IN 2006 TO PURSUE A WRITING CAREER IN NOVELS, TELEVISION, AND COMICS.